DATE DUE	RETURNED
OCT 0 2 2008	OCT 0 7 2008

CARIBOU

160201

Caribou

Michael Melski

Playwrights Canada Press
Toronto • Canada

Playwrights Canada Press
54 Wolseley St., 2nd floor Toronto, Ontario CANADA M5T 1A5
416-703-0013   fax 416-703-0059
orders@playwrightscanada.com • www.playwrightscanada.com

Playwrights Canada Press acknowledges the support of the taxpayers of Canada and the province of Ontario through The Canada Council for the Arts and the Ontario Arts Council.

Front cover design by Glen McMinn.
Production Editor: Jodi Armstrong

National Library of Canada Cataloguing in Publication

Melski, Michael, 1969-
    Caribou / Michael Melski.

A play.
ISBN 0-88754-690-0

    I. Title.

PS8576.E477C37 2003   C812'.54   C2003-903848-3

First edition: July 2003.
Printed and bound by AGMV Marquis at Quebec, Canada.

—•— Epigram —•—

*I've tasted my blood too much to abide
what I was born to.*

Milton Acorn

Caribou was first exhibited as a workshop production by the Stephenville Festival, Newfoundland, July 1995, as part of Brave New Works, with the following cast:

LOUIS   John Dartt
DUNCAN   Jerry Etienne

The production was directed by Allena MacDonald.

—•—

CARIBOU was given its first full production and provincial tour of Nova Scotia by Mulgrave Road Theatre Co-Op beginning March 17, 1998, with the following cast:

LOUIS   Michael Pellerin
DUNCAN   Hugh Thompson

The production was directed by Emmy Alcorn. Set designed by Darcy Poultney. Lighting by Kay MacDonald

—•—

The author wishes to acknowledge the dramaturgical contributions of all of the above, as well as Paula Danckert, Frank Flynn, Terrance Bryant, Rick Sherman, Steven Manuel, Philip Adams, and Yvette Nolan.

—•— Characters —•—

LOUIS   a man in his mid-thirties, average build.

DUNCAN   a man in his early-thirties, tall and heavy-set

—•— Time and Place —•—

A forest on a mountain. Rural Nova Scotia. The present.

Caribou

—•— Scene I —•—

Early morning. A dead-end dirt road at the foot of the mountain.

LOUIS	Ya have to hold it like this.
DUNCAN	Like this.
LOUIS	Now crack the breach.
DUNCAN	Crack the breach.
LOUIS	Leave it open. If we see somethin...
DUNCAN	Close it with the shell inside, shoot.
LOUIS	Steady. I'll tell ya when to do that.
DUNCAN	Anne said we might see a deer.
LOUIS	You just keep the safety on.
DUNCAN	Right.
LOUIS	Do ya know where the safety is?
DUNCAN	This.
LOUIS	That's the trigger.
DUNCAN	Shoot that.
LOUIS	No. You don't touch this little thing here.
DUNCAN	When?
LOUIS	*Ever.* You don't even breathe on it–
DUNCAN	I won't. Okay.

LOUIS   Don't even look at it, Duncan.

DUNCAN   Yeah.

LOUIS   Until I say it's okay. Very delicate. Ya got that?

DUNCAN   Got that.

LOUIS   Attaboy.

> *DUNCAN looks at it. LOUIS takes his rifle, and checks his sights.*

DUNCAN   Where are the shells?

LOUIS   I've got em. Don't worry.

DUNCAN   I carry the shells.

LOUIS   You don't need em yet.

DUNCAN   When?

LOUIS   When we see somethin.

> *Silence. DUNCAN looks at LOUIS.*

DUNCAN   Louis.

LOUIS   Yeah?

DUNCAN   I'm not supposed... take them down.

LOUIS   Take what down.

DUNCAN   Take those guns down from the fireplace. I...

LOUIS   Spit it out.

DUNCAN   I'm not supposed to shoot. I carry the shells.

LOUIS   Oh.

DUNCAN   The shells in the car from the hardware.

LOUIS   I see.

DUNCAN   I don't shoot the gun ever. Take it down ever.

LOUIS   Is that so?

DUNCAN   I could hurt something.

LOUIS   Yeah.

                    DUNCAN lays the shotgun on the ground.

DUNCAN   We could go home.

                    Pause.

LOUIS   Who said you're not allowed?

DUNCAN   My father and my mother.

LOUIS   Well, you know where they are, don't ya?

DUNCAN   They're in the graveyard.

LOUIS   That's right.

DUNCAN   Gone to heaven. Gone with the Lord.

LOUIS   So I say you can carry a rifle today. Pick it up.

DUNCAN   I don't know.

LOUIS   C'mon. You been buggin me to take you up here.

DUNCAN   Huntin.

LOUIS   Don't ya want to get a deer?

                    DUNCAN picks up the rifle.

DUNCAN   Okay.

LOUIS   Sit down till I finish gettin the gear ready.

DUNCAN	We can't take the truck no farther.
LOUIS	Run outta road. No road left.

LOUIS loads his rifle.

DUNCAN	Shoot something.
LOUIS	What did I say before?
DUNCAN	Shoot some cans. From the lunch bag.
LOUIS	When I say it's okay. Now...
DUNCAN	It's okay now.
LOUIS	No, it's not okay now. Just sit, Duncan.

LOUIS continues getting ready. DUNCAN points the gun toward LOUIS.

DUNCAN	Shoot you.

Pause.

LOUIS	Don't point that... watch you where y...!
DUNCAN	It's not loaded.
LOUIS	Ya point a gun at someone, the devil comes and puts a bullet in it.
DUNCAN	What?
LOUIS	Ever heard that one? The one about the devil?
DUNCAN	No.

Pause.

LOUIS	Maybe this isn't a good idea.
DUNCAN	I'm safe.

l to r: Hugh Thompson, Michael Pellerin. *Photo by Derek Hendsbee.*

LOUIS	...Go screwin around up here...
	Pause.
DUNCAN	I'm sorry, Louis.
LOUIS	You better be careful.
	Pause.
DUNCAN	We're going up on the mountain now.
LOUIS	You dressed warm enough there?
DUNCAN	Anne went lookin in the drawers. For underwear.
LOUIS	Good place for underwear.
DUNCAN	There was her wedding dress. In there.
LOUIS	Yeah?
DUNCAN	She showed it to me. It was in the basement.
LOUIS	Did the two a youse get married down there?
DUNCAN	*(pause)* No. We had a biscuit.
LOUIS	You never saw that dress before, huh?
	Pause.
DUNCAN	When your wedding was, I was at... gone away.
LOUIS	Oh yeah. That's right. Where were ya?
	Pause.
DUNCAN	I was at Selby then.
LOUIS	Yeah.

DUNCAN	I wasn't allowed to come home for it.
LOUIS	It's alright.
DUNCAN	Yeah, now. Anne promised.
LOUIS	She did. That she did.
DUNCAN	She promised my father. She wouldn't ever put me away there. At Selby.
LOUIS	I know. Cause of what ya did in there. I know.
DUNCAN	Yeah.

Pause.

LOUIS	Calm down.
DUNCAN	Ready.
LOUIS	Stay close. Walk in my steps.
DUNCAN	Walk in your steps.
LOUIS	And keep quiet.

They start to move along a path.

DUNCAN	I don't see any deer, Louis.

Pause.

LOUIS	No. There's no deer here *now*.
DUNCAN	Where are they?
LOUIS	We have to go *find* them.
DUNCAN	How?

LOUIS takes out a bottle. He drinks.

LOUIS	It takes patience. They're spooky. They never do what you expect. They're smarter than anyone thinks. But if you're patient enough, and smart enough, sometimes they come to you.

They continue out of sight, up the mountain.

—•— Scene 2 —•—

Late morning. An orchard.

LOUIS	They haunt this spot. They used to, anyway.
DUNCAN	Apples trees.
LOUIS	The deer eat them. Everythin turnin brown and it's too early for snow. Watch for a flash of white.

LOUIS scans the field.

DUNCAN	The deer aren't white.
LOUIS	Ya see white when a deer shows his rear-end. That's why they call them white tails.
DUNCAN	Shoot them in the ass.
LOUIS	No. Ya always pull a neck shot.
DUNCAN	Huh.
LOUIS	Don't worry about it.
DUNCAN	Show me.

LOUIS sets up DUNCAN with the gun.

LOUIS	Put the cross-hairs on the neck. *(pause)* Steady. Don't shoot for the head. You ruin the head, you can't mount the rack, an there's no trophy.
DUNCAN	Don't ruin the head. Mount the rack.

LOUIS	Can't aim low. A body shot won't drop him.
DUNCAN	Okay.
LOUIS	If I tell you to shoot, you just pull a neck shot.
DUNCAN	Kill him in the neck.

Pause.

LOUIS	And we better keep our eyes open, cause we might see someone around here.
DUNCAN	Who?
LOUIS	Some nosy fella. Game Warden. Some righteous bastard. Joe Curious. *Anyone....* Wants to know why we're huntin out of season.
DUNCAN	Joe Curious. Why are we huntin out of season?

Pause.

LOUIS	Cause we always do. It's tradition.
DUNCAN	Tradition.
LOUIS	If we run into some damn saint of the mountain, here's how we handle it. First, you let me do all the talkin...
DUNCAN	You do the talkin. Saint of the mountain.
LOUIS	If it's a warden, he's gonna ask to see your weapon.

LOUIS reaches for the gun. DUNCAN resists.

DUNCAN	It's mine.
LOUIS	You'll get it back, don't worry. Hand it to him stock first. Crack the breach like I showed ya. He'll say, "So fellas, what're you doin out here today?"
DUNCAN	Huntin.

LOUIS	What did I say? Don't say a goddamn word to him.
DUNCAN	What if he says somethin to me?
LOUIS	Just nod your head. This is the story. We were goin for a walk in the woods. Pick some apples to make jam.
DUNCAN	Bring the apples to Anne.
LOUIS	Good. Only keep your mouth shut. *(pause)* We saw this buck runnin down from the Glen Road. It was bleedin. Limpin. So we went back to the truck for the rifles. Gonna bring down that wounded deer.
DUNCAN	How did the deer get hurt?
LOUIS	*(pause)* He got hit by a car. Stubbed his Jesus toe.
DUNCAN	On a branch.
LOUIS	It *doesn't* matter. We gotta bring down that wounded deer. Because a wounded deer spreads its disease. A deer gets sick and spreads, it can destroy a population.
DUNCAN	A wounded deer spreads disease.
	Pause.
LOUIS	Then we followed the blood but we lost the trail.
DUNCAN	Followed the blood. Lost the trail.
LOUIS	That's the story we're gonna tell.
DUNCAN	Okay.
	DUNCAN practices with his gun. LOUIS takes out a bottle and opens it.
LOUIS	You like stories, don't ya Duncan.
DUNCAN	Anne tells me stories in the cabin.

LOUIS	I know she does. You like the cabin?
DUNCAN	I always keep the cabin clean.
LOUIS	Well, I know my friend wants to be in his own place doesn't he? That's why we gave up the backyard.
DUNCAN	Yeah.

LOUIS drinks.

LOUIS	Havin a good time?
DUNCAN	I like huntin.
LOUIS	Well, you need more exercise. Anne thinks it's the cause a' your roamin around lately.

Pause.

DUNCAN	I don't know.
LOUIS	So what happened down by the school the other day?

Silence.

DUNCAN	Nothin.
LOUIS	*(laughs)* Innocent as can be.
DUNCAN	We already talked about it, Louis.
LOUIS	It's just us now, and I want the straight goods.
DUNCAN	Straight goods.
LOUIS	I don't like to do anything until I see all sides of a thing. I don't see all the sides.

Pause.

You tell the truth now. No one else can hear.

Silence.

DUNCAN I was just up there.

LOUIS You were. And you broke the rules. You know you're not supposed to walk on the highway.

DUNCAN I cross over the road. To Mackie's house.

LOUIS Crossin the road is one thing. Walkin it is another. It's the fuckin Trans-Canada *highway,* Duncan.

DUNCAN I hate the fuckin big trucks.

LOUIS And you know you're not supposed to go in town without us. Last time, you sat down for a good spell.

DUNCAN I had to sit down in the cabin.

LOUIS So I ask, if you don't like the trucks, and you don't like the sit-down for breakin the rules, then somethin pretty strong must have made you want to go in town there.

Pause.

DUNCAN That day. I went in town to find Anne.

LOUIS Anne doesn't work anywhere near the school.

Pause.

What in the name of God were you doin down back of the schoolyard where those kids were?

DUNCAN I went a shortcut.

LOUIS You went a shortcut.

DUNCAN Through the woods. Everyone does the shortcut.

LOUIS Well, you're not everyone.

DUNCAN Yeah.

LOUIS	So Anne has to call me at work, doesn't she. And I have to explain to my foreman. What am I supposed to say? I have to leave the job site cause my brother-in-law's wandering around the schoolyard up to God knows what. Doesn't sound too good. Doesn't matter what I say in your defence, cause you know how word spreads around here. Like a goddamn forest fire. And now some people are pretty pissed off with us.
DUNCAN	I was just there.
LOUIS	Two kids told everyone in town you were starin.

Pause.

DUNCAN	I saw them. That's all.

Pause.

LOUIS	See, I know what those kids do down there. That's where they go to smoke grass. Feel each other up. Get their first blow jobs. I went there. Everyone knows. You know too. Were those kids up to business?
DUNCAN	*(pause)* I don't know. I went to find Anne.
LOUIS	You weren't lookin for somethin else?

Silence.

What the hell are you doin? You got everythin you need in the cabin... we leave the doors to the house open. Who are you goin to see in town?

DUNCAN thinks. LOUIS returns to his bottle.

DUNCAN	Louis. I look for you.

Pause.

LOUIS	You look for me..

Pause.

DUNCAN   I want to do like you. Go in town like you. In the woods like you. *(pause)* I don't want to stay in the cabin all the time. I don't want to be... a dirty secret. No more.

Silence.

LOUIS   You want to be like me.

LOUIS drinks.

DUNCAN   Tuesday. Wednesday. Your days off in town. I know.

Pause.

LOUIS   I get a call like that at work. I shouldn't *ever* have to get a call like that at work.

DUNCAN   I'm sorry.

LOUIS   People start talking. A bad name follows you. It follows your whole family. And you know what we got comin. We got the little one coming soon, don't we?

DUNCAN   The baby.

LOUIS   And what you Duncan do today is gonna follow our little baby its whole life. Do you follow me?

DUNCAN   I can make things better. For the baby.

Pause.

LOUIS   There's gotta be changes. Big changes. I don't think you might like them very much.

DUNCAN   Okay, Louis.

LOUIS gathers his gear. He watches DUNCAN.

LOUIS   Sometimes I wonder about you.

Pause.

Maybe you're not so incapable. Maybe you know exactly what you're doin, just how much you can get away with. The right thing to say to get yourself out of trouble. Isn't that right?

DUNCAN   I don't know, Louis.

LOUIS slings his rifle.

LOUIS   People should know what they are.

DUNCAN slings his shotgun as LOUIS does. The men leave the orchard.

— • — Scene 3 — • —

Mid afternoon. A hardwood ridge.

LOUIS   Scat's still warm. Fresh track.

DUNCAN   Shit.

LOUIS   There's a ten pointer around this stand. Got a shot off at him once when I was with Mackie.

Pause.

DUNCAN   Louis.

LOUIS   What?

DUNCAN   Piss now.

LOUIS   We're right on fuckin top of one, Duncan.

DUNCAN   I gotta go.

LOUIS   Hold it.

DUNCAN   Nature rules.

> *DUNCAN moves into the woods.*

LOUIS Fuck. Get away from the trail. Stay downwind.

> *Silence. LOUIS scans the trees.*

Hurry up.

> *Pause. LOUIS hears a strange sound.*

Is there a problem?

> *Pause.*

DUNCAN I can't zip the zipper back.

LOUIS Why not?

DUNCAN It's stuck. My hands are frozen.

LOUIS What happened to your gloves?

DUNCAN I don't know.

LOUIS *(pause)* What the hell do you expect me to do?

DUNCAN I can't feel my hands.

LOUIS Stick em in your pockets. Warm em up.

> *Pause.*

DUNCAN It's cold in my pockets too.

LOUIS Just forget it. Fly free. Let's go.

DUNCAN I'll frostbite my dick. The wind goes in.

LOUIS Duncan, if you can't do up your own fly, you got no right bein here. No right bein anywhere, but...

> *LOUIS takes off his gloves and moves to DUNCAN. He starts to work the zipper.*

Merciful heaven, that's *disgusting.*

DUNCAN   What?

LOUIS   Don't give me that. You know!

> *DUNCAN laughs.*

DUNCAN   When it gets too big, Louis. I can't zip.

LOUIS   It's not fucking funny. Shut up.

DUNCAN   Sorry.

> *DUNCAN tries to stop. Silence.*

LOUIS   You wanted to show me, didn't ya?

DUNCAN   Huh.

> *Pause.*

LOUIS   You were playin with yourself.

DUNCAN   No.

LOUIS   Maybe you're on the queer side. You want to fuck me?

DUNCAN   Yeah. Fuck you.

> *DUNCAN laughs.*

LOUIS   Or maybe you just get off on fucking *with* me.

DUNCAN   I was just havin a piss.

LOUIS   You like that cock of yours. You want to show it around. I don't blame ya. A cock that big should have its own area code. Maybe you don't like anyone tellin you what the rules are. Eh?

> *No response.*

Who else you been showin it to, I wonder.

Pause.

DUNCAN   I keep it in my pants. What you're supposed to do.

LOUIS   *(laughs)* I know the fuckin lay of the land.

DUNCAN   Huh.

LOUIS   It's all makin sense now. You're in heat. Duncan's in heat.

LOUIS laughs.

DUNCAN   I'm not in heat. I'm fucking cold.

LOUIS   That's why all the roamin around. Visitin you call it. Down the road to town. Behind the school. Across to Mackies. You're looking to get a taste.

Pause.

This changes things.

DUNCAN   I go visitin. I don't have to stay in the cabin.

LOUIS drinks.

LOUIS   You like goin over Mackie's a lot, don't ya.

DUNCAN   Yeah. I go there.

LOUIS   You aren't doin what we told you never to do?

DUNCAN   I don't go near the dogs.

LOUIS   So why do you like goin there so much?

DUNCAN   I like crossin over the road.

LOUIS   Uh-huh. Sure. Looking over Mackie's wife. That's what. Goin to see Peg. That's what you're doin.

LOUIS passes DUNCAN the bottle. He takes it.

DUNCAN	I go in the kitchen with her.
LOUIS	*(laughs)* Someone's in the kitchen with Peg.
DUNCAN	We have tea in there.
LOUIS	Tea. And what else?
DUNCAN	We play cards.
LOUIS	What kind?
DUNCAN	Fish.

LOUIS laughs. DUNCAN laughs with him.

LOUIS	Lots of fellas wouldn't mind playin a few hands with her. Who else you been visitin?
DUNCAN	No one.
LOUIS	Well, you're goin in town all the time now.
DUNCAN	Are we gonna hunt or or are we gonna talk?
LOUIS	This is better than huntin.
DUNCAN	Yeah.
LOUIS	I envy you. Guy's got nothing better to do all day than roam around, play cards, sip fuckin tea and admire your cock. You kinda got an ideal lifestyle, you know that?
DUNCAN	I hate my life.

Pause.

LOUIS	You play with yourself a lot. Out in the cabin?
DUNCAN	No.
LOUIS	It's alright. You can't control yourself.

DUNCAN   It's a sin, Louis.

LOUIS   Don't give me that. It's normal as grass.

DUNCAN   Huh?

LOUIS   *(snaps)* I ain't fuckin stupid. I never bought a Pontiac.

DUNCAN   I'm not playin dumb. I am dumb...

LOUIS   Like hell ya are. You're *devious*.

    Pause.

    Maybe you can hide from other people. But I watch you. I know more than you think. I'm a little slow myself but I build things. I put pieces together, and I don't like what I see.

DUNCAN   What?

LOUIS   I don't care what you do out in the cabin. It's your place. It's probably a good thing you found your dick. A man should probably find his dick before he's forty. It's funny in a way. Duncan's in heat. It's mad funny.

    DUNCAN laughs.

DUNCAN   Yeah.

LOUIS   What isn't so funny is what's goin on beneath our window some nights. It's you. Muckin up the flowerbed.

    Pause.

DUNCAN   I'm going to the fridge. In your house.

LOUIS   Cause I don't really give a sweet shit if you're out in the cabin beatin your leather. It'd be unreasonable if I gave a shit about that. What you do out there.

DUNCAN   Midnight snack, Louis. I'm goin to eat...

LOUIS   But it is reasonable for me to be concerned about what goes on underneath my window. And Anne sure wouldn't care much about what a grown man does in private. *(pause)*

But you aren't bein so private anymore.

DUNCAN   I'm hungry.

LOUIS   You are. And now we have a dangerous situation.

Pause.

Maybe I should listen to what some people say. Sooner or later, you're going to hurt someone.

DUNCAN   I never hurt anyone.

LOUIS   Not yet. *(pause)* You know how many kids live around our area? I know you do. I've got to be able to assure my neighbours that those kids are safe walkin by my damn house.

DUNCAN   I'm safe.

LOUIS   Are they? I talked to the bus driver. He said he always sees you by the road when he's droppin the kids off.

Silence.

DUNCAN   I wave to the bus. It comes on time.

LOUIS   I bet. What do you wave at them?

DUNCAN   I wave to the bus. It always...

LOUIS   You like the kids.

DUNCAN   The kids don't... like me... they... *(pause)* Go away.

LOUIS   That's what you were doin down by the school. Playin with yourself. Watchin the kids.

Silence.

DUNCAN   It was them.

LOUIS   Don't lie.

Pause.

DUNCAN   They put their hands down their pants. The boy and the girl. Both. They laid down. On top of her. Behind the school there. I saw them. I was just there. They did it.

LOUIS drinks.

LOUIS   What do ya think Anne would say about all this?

Silence.

DUNCAN   Don't tell.

LOUIS   She has to know about it.

DUNCAN   No.

LOUIS   Maybe the baby's not safe.

DUNCAN   The baby's safe. I never hurt...

LOUIS   What do you think should happen?

DUNCAN   Don't tell Anne, Louis!

Pause.

LOUIS   Something's gotta be done. Something has to change. I don't have to tell her squat if we can come up with a better idea... I don't know. Only thing I can think of is you gotta take yourself out of harm's way...

Silence.

DUNCAN   If you tell Anne, I'll tell what you did.

LOUIS   Huh?

Pause.

DUNCAN   You go visitin. I know. You go in town.

Silence.

LOUIS   What the fuck are you talkin about?

DUNCAN   You go visitin... Janie.

Pause.

I saw you. The truck by her house.

LOUIS   You didn't see a goddamn thing.

DUNCAN   You came outside. In the truck. You were with her.

LOUIS drinks.

LOUIS   I dropped over there one day to give her a hand movin furniture.

DUNCAN   Two days. You gave her money.

LOUIS   Doesn't mean a thing. And so what if it does? What *right* do you have to be meddlin in my private business...? You aren't even supposed to *be* in town!

DUNCAN   Anne loves you.

DUNCAN rises.

LOUIS   Shut up.

DUNCAN   Don't tell Anne, Louis. Don't.

Silence. LOUIS looks at DUNCAN.

LOUIS	Guess I underestimated you. I'm sorry about that. I been tryin hard to solve this somehow. We should handle this more like friends. Huh? What do ya say?
DUNCAN	Friends.

Pause.

LOUIS	You know who Janie Boyd is, Duncan. What she does? I'll take you to see her.
DUNCAN	What do you mean?
LOUIS	I'll take ya over town, get ya fixed up. Some day when Anne is over Inverness for her check-up.
DUNCAN	I go see Janie.
LOUIS	Janie Boyd. She's a pretty lady.
DUNCAN	Yeah.
LOUIS	She'll do some things to you. Oh, will she do some things to you. *(laughs)* We could sell tickets to that.
DUNCAN	What will she do to me?
LOUIS	Unspeakable things. She'll jump your bones.

Silence.

DUNCAN	No.
LOUIS	Why not? C'mon. It's somethin good. Don't you want to enjoy a little flesh in your hand besides your own? I'm tryin to do right by you.

Pause.

DUNCAN	I don't love her. I love Anne.
LOUIS	It's a different kind of love, Duncan.

DUNCAN   Anne...

LOUIS   Anne doesn't have to know about these things, does she? *(pause)* It'll be our secret.

DUNCAN   I don't want to be with her... like Anne.

Silence.

LOUIS   Hangin around the little sister your whole life. You got a lot of wrong ideas, my friend. *(pause)* What are ya. A boy or a girl?

DUNCAN   Huh.

LOUIS spars lightly but with intent.

LOUIS   Don't ya want to get laid for once? Where ya at? Which one are ya? Girl or a boy? Do ya know?

DUNCAN   I know where...

LOUIS   Show me which one ya are. C'mon.

DUNCAN   I live at number six-seven oh two Hornes Road Route...

LOUIS   What're ya sayin? Did I ask for our address?

DUNCAN   I'm thirty-six in June, my birthday is in June Our father who art in heaven...

LOUIS   Prayin now. Christ almighty...

DUNCAN   I KNOW WHERE I LIVE, LOUIS! I KNOW...!

DUNCAN stops just short of attacking him. LOUIS retreats.

LOUIS   Try to get you fixed up a little. That's the thanks I get.

DUNCAN   Don't... fuck with me.

LOUIS   I offer you a chance for some love for the first time,
         what do you do? Take my head off for it. Go off
         half-cocked on *me*. *(pause)* I take you up here.
         I show ya things. I don't go shootin off to Anne
         about half of what I know cause I want to hear your
         side. Who else did so much? Who cared? Duncan?
         What dumb shit even tried? You're not my blood,
         your sister promised to care for you, I wasn't there
         at the time. But I'm here now, pissin in the wind.

              Pause.

DUNCAN   So am I.

LOUIS   Maybe it's hopeless. Maybe there's only one way it
         can be.

              Silence.

DUNCAN   Louis.

LOUIS   What?

DUNCAN   I want to.

LOUIS   Huh.

              Pause.

DUNCAN   I want to stick it in sometimes. Squeeze it in...
         sometimes.

LOUIS   Yeah?

DUNCAN   And when it gets hard, then I lay on them.

LOUIS   *(pause)* You lay on them, do ya. Ya get laid?

DUNCAN   Yeah. Lay on them. Fuck them.

LOUIS   You know how, don't ya.

              *DUNCAN straddles a log and thrusts his hips
              violently.*

DUNCAN	Yeah.... Yeah...
LOUIS	You animal. Give it to her.
DUNCAN	Give it to her. Give it to her.

Pause.

| LOUIS | You fucking animal. |

—•— Scene 4 —•—

Late afternoon. A spruce grove.

DUNCAN practices with the rifle. LOUIS drinks. Faraway.

DUNCAN Put the crosshairs on the neck. Crack the breach. No. Click the safety. Ready. Aim. Feet apart. Don't shoot for the head. Steady...

Pause.

LOUIS You're staring at it too long. If you get one lined up, you can't stare forever. Ya start seein Bambi.

DUNCAN Bambi. Huh.

LOUIS It's a game animal. Menace to the roads, crops. Cull the herd for the good of the herd. The strong ones make it through winter. The weak starve out.

DUNCAN lines up the target.

DUNCAN Thou shalt not kill.

LOUIS What?

DUNCAN Thou shalt not kill... Bambi.

DUNCAN shoots. The firing pin clicks.

LOUIS Have a slug. It'll help your courage.

DUNCAN takes it.

DUNCAN Thanks.

Pause.

LOUIS First one's the hardest. Once ya make a first kill, ya see how easy it is. It's a miracle we all don't kill each other. Gut each other in the streets.

Pause.

DUNCAN What's guttin?

LOUIS Don't worry your pretty little head about it.

DUNCAN I want to know.

Pause. LOUIS uses a knife to demonstrate.

LOUIS After you make a kill,you slit its throat. Bleed it. Then you open it up underneath and spill the guts so it doesn't ruin the meat. But everything's attached in there. You have to reach inside with your bare hands and cut all the connections.

DUNCAN Uh-huh.

Pause.

LOUIS Then we gotta get the heart. We save the heart.

DUNCAN The heart.

LOUIS Don't make a pussy face. This is what happens. We have to bring the heart back for Joe The Chinaman.

DUNCAN What does he do with it?

LOUIS Joe the Chinaman *eats* the fuckin hearts.

Silence.

DUNCAN We could go home.

LOUIS	This is prime huntin time. We're almost at the top. Can't leave without lookin at the bare patch.
	Pause.
DUNCAN	I don't have to gut the deer, Louis.
LOUIS	Everyone guts their own. That's tradition.
DUNCAN	Tradition.
	Silence.
LOUIS	Do ya know why we're gonna bring the heart back for old Joe? That's another tradition.
DUNCAN	Okay.
LOUIS	You heard that word lots of times.
	Pause.
DUNCAN	Christmas.
LOUIS	Yeah. Good fella. You like Christmas?
DUNCAN	Yeah.
LOUIS	You like traditions, then.
DUNCAN	Okay.
	LOUIS passes him the bottle. DUNCAN drinks.
LOUIS	It's something that always happens. Anybody around here gets a deer, they always bring the heart back for the Chinaman. He's freaky as fuckin Friday. Guts his deer with a samurai blade and eats the stuff other people throw away. No one fucks with him, and no one gets a deer around here without givin him the heart. Doesn't make sense at all. Sometimes, the only explanation is tradition.
DUNCAN	Yeah.

LOUIS	Like you out in your cabin. It's traditional for a person to want a shelter of their own.
DUNCAN	Anne takes my supper to the cabin.
LOUIS	Yeah. Your sister gives you the royal treatment. I don't mind you makin us wait for dinner or she goes outside when you get scared at night.
DUNCAN	Before she married you , she stayed every night.

Pause.

LOUIS	She feels sorry for ya. So do I. Out in the backyard all night. You're alone in the world.
DUNCAN	I'm not alone with her.

Silence.

LOUIS	Fair enough. We want ya to have the best possible home. You deserve that, with the crosses you got...
DUNCAN	Anne is my home.
LOUIS	But with everythin that's goin on since you been livin with us, I have to ask myself... are we failin ya? I mean is what we can provide the best possible home for Duncan? Maybe we aren't qualified to give ya what ya deserve. And with the changes we got comin.... Y'understand me?
DUNCAN	Uh-huh.
LOUIS	I'm sayin maybe you need a different *kind* of cabin.
DUNCAN	What kind of cabin.
LOUIS	Everyone needs to be in a place where they're safe.
DUNCAN	I'm safe.
LOUIS	That's the most important thing about a home. A person's gotta feel safe in their home. A person's gotta be safe. An that's the thing of it, Duncan.

DUNCAN	What?

Pause.

LOUIS I'm sayin,, there are traditions about where people who are sick... who are not right, about where their home is. *(pause)* Maybe Selby is where you're more safe. Maybe that's more your home.

Silence.

DUNCAN I don't have to go to Selby.

LOUIS I'm not saying you have to, but maybe you don't understand. How it's not such a bad place.

DUNCAN I don't have to... with Anne, Louis.

LOUIS Hey. Everyone's tried their best. It's our failure as much as yours. But we have to face realities.

DUNCAN Anne promised.

LOUIS There's decent people who run it. They take good care. They know *how*...

DUNCAN Anne promised... my father...

LOUIS Settle down. Listen to me a sec...

DUNCAN *I can't...*

Pause.

LOUIS Duncan. I know you were a danger to yourself when you were in there. *(pause)* But you're a danger when you're not in there. And you might be a danger to others too, the way things have been going lately. I hope not, but we don't know, do we? An accident only has to happen once. *(pause)* And you're a danger to us, too. To me and Anne. Do ya know that?

DUNCAN I'm not a danger to Anne.

LOUIS   Maybe you don't know how, but you are.

DUNCAN   How?

> *Pause.*

LOUIS   You remember when I was going out with your sister. Before we were married?

DUNCAN   Yeah.

LOUIS   Before you went...

DUNCAN   You had nice shoes on.

LOUIS   *(laughs)* I did, did I?

DUNCAN   You always gave her flowers.

LOUIS   That's right.

DUNCAN   Then she gave them to me.

> *Pause.*

LOUIS   Maybe that's why you had such a problem when we got serious with things. When you made it so hard for her. Your parents had to send you away.

DUNCAN   I didn't want you to take her.

> *Pause.*

LOUIS   I know ya didn't. But I'd do anything for Anne's happiness. That's what I told your parents when I asked for her hand. Would you?

DUNCAN   Yeah.

LOUIS   Don't you want your sister to be happy?

DUNCAN   Anne was happy. Before.

> *Pause.*

LOUIS	Do you ever wonder why your sister married me? Out of all the fellas comin around?
DUNCAN	No.
LOUIS	Me either. I wasn't the smartest, or the handsomest. For a long time, I thought I was just the luckiest.
DUNCAN	Yeah.
LOUIS	The main reason your sister married me was because I can *provide* for her. Know what that means?
DUNCAN	Get things.
LOUIS	That's right. *Everythin* she needs.

Pause.

DUNCAN	Uh-huh.
LOUIS	I take decent care of your sister, don't I.
DUNCAN	You take care of her.

Pause.

LOUIS	And I take care of you too, now. Cause you can't provide for yourself. You gotta be with people who can provide for you, right? So I provide for two.
DUNCAN	Three. You provide for you.
LOUIS	Very good. Cause Anne's not going to be able to work full-time once she gets the baby. And you had that litter-picker job that didn't work out.
DUNCAN	I didn't like to stay so long.
LOUIS	Well, eight hours is a long time to be away from your sweetie. But what happens is, I gotta be at work even more to make the money to provide.

So I'm not around much. I'm taking care of you both – and she's takin care of you. It's pretty comfy.

DUNCAN Yeah.

LOUIS For some. Except while I'm out there on that road crew a hundred clicks away, twelve hours a day sometimes, I can't concentrate. Cause I'm thinkin bad things.

Pause.

I'm thinkin what'll happen if Anne has an emergency and I'm too far away to help? What if she takes a fall while she's playin some game with you, chasin you around? What if that happens and I can't be there? She could die.

DUNCAN Anne won't die. I'm with her.

LOUIS She could. The baby could. I get horrible thoughts. Like jackhammers. I try to keep them out, but they won't stay out.

DUNCAN I help her. Do the chores. I know.

LOUIS It's no substitute for me being home more often. If I was workin to support two that could happen. What's going to happen when there's four?

DUNCAN Louis. I never let her... hurt.

LOUIS Look at you. Can't keep your clothes tucked in. Lost your mitts. Can't even zip your zipper. If you can't handle those little things, how you gonna handle it when she's hemorrhaging all over the place? I should be there. I *could* be there if...

DUNCAN I know Emergency. Nine-one-one. Ambulance. Six-seven-zero-four-two-three-five. Firetruck.

LOUIS There's other things, too, that can happen.

DUNCAN Four-six-five-six. Police. Six-seven-zero...

LOUIS	When a husband is forced to be away from his wife!
DUNCAN	I can protect Anne, Louis.
LOUIS	You can't protect her if you're damaging us!
DUNCAN	How.

LOUIS offers DUNCAN the bottle. Pause.

LOUIS	I love your sister. She's the only woman I've ever loved. It's the... certain love ya get in your stomach and ya can't eat? And all you do is think about how beautiful she is an how lucky you are, and how it's a miracle.
DUNCAN	Me and Anne.
LOUIS	No! I'm talking about deep love between two human beings. It's beautiful. It's unexplainable. It's fragile.
DUNCAN	Fragile.
LOUIS	Means ya gotta *protect* it.
DUNCAN	I know.
LOUIS	Ya think ya do. *(pause)* If I can't be near my wife enough than I gotta spend even more time to make things right between us. Cause you know what they say about absence, Duncan?
DUNCAN	What.
LOUIS	Absence makes the eyes wander. Tell me this. Does Mackie ever come by in the middle of the day?

Pause.

DUNCAN	I didn't see anyone.
LOUIS	Think hard. Do ya ever see any men from town come to visit Anne when I'm not home?

DUNCAN   No, Louis.

LOUIS   Cause you know what I'd do to a fella who did that.

DUNCAN   What.

LOUIS drinks.

LOUIS   You wouldn't tell me anyway. See, it's very difficult to be living with a person ya don't trust. *(pause)* I'm not too worried. She's got a kid on the way so she's not goin anywhere very far. Not yet anyway *(pause)* Not hearin too much under the window lately, are ya? And don't get me started on that! I'm talkin here about the damage *already* done... so...

DUNCAN   So what.

LOUIS   What I'm sayin is... it's pretty damn hard to do the makin things right when you got a... guy like you around and it's eatin up our life. Eatin up that time when you can repair the damage done in the natural course of things. Wouldn't ya say?

Pause.

I'd say it's traditional for a husband and wife to have a little time together. Like maybe a few minutes alone at home at night. I get home every day after trying my best to provide for my expectant wife, so we can bring a child into the world, into a better life. *What kinda life?* Serve Duncan and wash Duncan and clean Duncan's mess and explain things to Duncan. My whole fuckin life revolves around you and what you need.

DUNCAN   Uh-huh.

LOUIS   One of you oughta explain somethin to me... where the hell do I fit?! I'm a goddamn outsider in my own house, that I built with my hands! *(spits)* A fuckin patsy. *(pause)* If I was a stronger man, maybe I could walk out on the whole mess.

DUNCAN	Yeah. You could.

Pause.

LOUIS	You'd like that.

Pause.

DUNCAN	I could take care of her.
LOUIS	Ya think so.
DUNCAN	Better than you.
LOUIS	Ya deluded bastard. You're gonna support a woman and child? Ya can't pick trash off the ground.

Pause.

DUNCAN	Before you came, we were family together. Me and Anne. Now you want me back to Selby. Before you came... Anne never said... back to Selby.
LOUIS	Well, Anne doesn't always know what's best. I've been hopin that you might realize it. I was a fool to try.
DUNCAN	The best was before. Anne changed. She went with you. I learned to hate.

Pause.

Anne said not to hate. God says. I try.

LOUIS	To think I felt sorry for you. You want this to happen. Drive me out of my own home.

Pause.

DUNCAN	I watch. What you do. Louis.
LOUIS	Yeah. I know what you like to watch.
DUNCAN	To Janie's. Everywhere. I follow you.

LOUIS	Follow me around town. You're *stalkin* me then.
DUNCAN	I watch. So I can know things. How to do like you. Everythin like you. Hunt like you. Provide. Kill.
LOUIS	Ya demented fuck. Think you can scare me?
DUNCAN	No, Louis.

> *Silence.*

My sister loves you.

LOUIS	Sure she does.

> *DUNCAN moves toward him and offers back the bottle. Pause.*

DUNCAN	You're my brother.
LOUIS	Brother-in-law, ya mean.

> *Pause.*

DUNCAN	Brother.

> *Silence. LOUIS takes the bottle.*

> *The sun is beginning to set.*

—•— Scene 5 —•—

> *Early evening. Near the top of the mountain.*

> *LOUIS is wasted, singing loudly.*

DUNCAN	Louis?

> *LOUIS keeps singing.*

Over there. I heard somethin.

LOUIS	Sure ya did.

DUNCAN	Maybe it was a deer.
LOUIS	Ya heard a deer, huh. They were attracted by the singing maybe? What a piece a work you are.
DUNCAN	It was there. It was somethin big.
LOUIS	*(laughs)* Some fuckin caribou jumped off the quarter in my pocket, he needed to take a piss.
DUNCAN	It was right in the bushes. There.

LOUIS grabs the barrel of DUNCAN's rifle.

LOUIS	What did I tell ya about tell ya about pointin that rod in my direction?
DUNCAN	Let go.
LOUIS	Y'know how many fellas get killed cause some village idiot goes blastin away at sound in the bushes?
DUNCAN	Let it go.

Pause. LOUIS releases it.

LOUIS	Ha. You should blow my head off. I had to be brain damaged myself to let this go on as long as this. It's my own fuckin fault for bein a weakling.

LOUIS opens another bottle.

DUNCAN	Maybe we should go home.
LOUIS	No way. We're at the top of the hill now. Didn't come all this way just to to turn around. We came up here to do somethin. To fix a problem.
DUNCAN	We could go chase that deer.

LOUIS starts to laugh.

LOUIS	There aren't any fuckin deer up here.

DUNCAN   Huh.

LOUIS   Between my old man, Joe the Chinaman and the
               Indians in Middle River, you'd be lucky if you found
               a white tail within twenty miles of here.

DUNCAN   Louis...?

LOUIS   Maybe one or two wander through once in a while.
               Dogs run em down, eat them while they're still
               alive...

DUNCAN   There's no deer.

               DUNCAN rises. LOUIS rises with him.

LOUIS   Hey. You know why Mackie's dog bit ya that time.

DUNCAN   No.

LOUIS   Liar. Of course you do.

DUNCAN   He bit me cause he's mad.

LOUIS   He wasn't mad. I never got the chance to speak
               about this because Anne took it outta my hands.

DUNCAN   He's a mad dog.

LOUIS   You were teasin the dog, that's why.

DUNCAN   I never teased him.

LOUIS   Well, you're a lyin little bugger aren't ya. I saw ya
               tease the dog. Pokin at him with a stick.

DUNCAN   No. I wasn't...

LOUIS   Just like with me. Torment me.

DUNCAN   Anne knows. Peg knows. About the dog.

LOUIS   Yeah. Little blood on Percy I had to shut up on that
               whole business. I never got a word in. Between

Anne and Peg, you got both those women snowed. The women love you, eh. Why's that, I suppose?

DUNCAN   I don't know.

LOUIS   Bullshit. All we've done for ya and ya lie every chance you get. Five hundred dollar dog got put down cause your lie that time... good neighbor...

Pause.

What's it gonna be next time? What're ya gonna poke to death next time?

Pause.

Whole town's either laughin at us or scared of us. I got no neighbors. No dignity anymore in front of anyone. Not even my own wife, whose stupid promises made this situation.

LOUIS drinks.

DUNCAN   Anne's makin supper now. It's time.

LOUIS   Your supper's twenty miles walk away from here. You're gonna need a pretty long fuckin fork.

DUNCAN   I'm goin myself, Louis.

Pause.

LOUIS   It'll be dark in a half-hour. You don't want to get lost up here. Last fella got lost up here. They never found him for ten years. He was nothin but bones in a red jacket by then.

DUNCAN   I'm goin home with Anne.

LOUIS follows him.

LOUIS   Look at you. Spoiled ya rotten, she has. Yeah, she'll warm up your mittens for ya. C'mere.

DUNCAN	No.
LOUIS	C'mere. Stand up to me.
DUNCAN	Fuck you.

LOUIS slaps DUNCAN across the face.

LOUIS	Ooh. Look at those eyes. You're scary, Duncan. Want some more? Think I'm scareda you?
DUNCAN	Don't.
LOUIS	Why not. I took my licks. I'm still takin em.
DUNCAN	Never... hit me! Never...!
LOUIS	Don't worry. It won't ever happen again. I'm through pussy-footin around with you!
DUNCAN	Good!
LOUIS	Tomorrow morning, you're going back to Selby where ya rightly belong.

Silence.

Me and Anne decided this.

DUNCAN	Huh?
LOUIS	She wanted me to take ya up here. Thought it would make it easier if you were away from her.

Pause.

DUNCAN	Anne. Anne said.

Silence.

LOUIS	There ain't gonna be no fuss about it either. It's been hard enough on the poor girl. There ain't gonna be no big screamin scenes cause that ain't gonna work anymore.

l to r: Michael Pellerin, Hugh Thompson. *Photo by Derek Hendsbee.*

DUNCAN   Anne. Anne...

LOUIS   When we go down there, you're gonna tell Anne that you're ready to go back. You want to go back.

DUNCAN   Go back... Anne... I...

LOUIS   If you never heard me today at all, listen to me now. This is somethin you gotta take like a man. The world isn't a big cuppa tea, y'know, for anyone. This has to happen for the good of everyone and everything. And you're going to show everyone that you're a big enough man to accept it.

DUNCAN   Why... Louis?

LOUIS   Because we say so. That's why. Because *I* fuckin say so, too. Because I work too hard for that not to count.

DUNCAN   ...Promised. My father... and my mother... she...

LOUIS   That's all over now.

> *DUNCAN looks at him.*

DUNCAN   You. You told her. You told.... You...

LOUIS   This is the best thing we can do. To protect you and us. It isn't an easy thing. But it's the best thing.

DUNCAN   I... I never hurt Anne. She... promised me.

> *Pause.*

LOUIS   Cry if ya want an I know ya will cause you're a cute bastard an ya learned how to get what you want. Cry all ya want about it but you're gonna see... mark my words... and later you'll appreciate because ya love Anne cause me and Anne did a damn good job with you, besides... *(drinks)* It's not my problem is it. Not my fuckin promise... promises *somethin*.... Yeah? Not my problem if your people take their vows right down to goddamn grave with them. My people can't take vows down the driveway to put out the fuckin garbage garbage day. I don't make that anyone else's problem, do I. Do I?

DUNCAN is silent.

I kept the promise longer than anyone would, anyone else would have... any name... Sure. Honour the dead. Fine. The dead are honoured. I just hope that when I'm dead I'll be as lucky as them.

DUNCAN   I don't want to go there.

LOUIS   One of us is goin there. An if it isn't you, it's gonna be me before long... Get it out of your system. I don't want you cryin in front of your sister.

DUNCAN   I don't want to go there, Louis.

Pause.

LOUIS   You'll have all those pretty nurses waitin on ya. It's not gonna be so bad. And we're gonna visit ya too. Every weekend or so we'll come visit. I promise.

DUNCAN   No...

LOUIS   Say it's okay, Duncan. *(pause)* Ya say it's okay.

Pause.

DUNCAN   I don't go to Selby.

LOUIS   Ya don't, huh?

DUNCAN   I don't... have to go to Selby.

LOUIS   Ohh. You don't *have* to go Selby.

DUNCAN   At Selby, they... they have...

LOUIS   Hmm?

DUNCAN   They got... there... at Sel...

LOUIS	What. What do they have there?
DUNCAN	There... th...
LOUIS	What do they got there? Retards? Is that what they got at Selby? Retards, Duncan?
DUNCAN	Fences... they got high *fences*... at...
LOUIS	Sure they do, Duncan. That's to keep the retards in.
DUNCAN	You're not allowed... they scream... everyone screams.
LOUIS	Listen to ya. That's how people know where the retards are. That's so normal people know to stay the fuck away if they want. If we didn't have Selby with the fences, we wouldn't need normal would we?

Silence. DUNCAN rises.

DUNCAN	No Louis.
LOUIS	What?
DUNCAN	Anne said.

Pause.

LOUIS	What are ya sayin?
DUNCAN	Anne promised.
LOUIS	It's closed, Duncan. There's no more promise.
DUNCAN	Anne won't make ya... won't make ya put me in there.... She said... Anne said.
LOUIS	Sorry. She didn't say fuck all else.
DUNCAN	I know she said. I know she said. I know.
LOUIS	Ya know nothin.

DUNCAN   I know she said! I know!

                Pause.

                You said. You.

LOUIS   What. Ya callin me a liar?

DUNCAN   Anne said... Selby never.

LOUIS   You're callin me a liar then!

DUNCAN   LIAR! LIES! LIAR! You said. Anne never said... Anne said never. You said.... YOU...!

                Silence.

LOUIS   And you're not a liar yourself.

DUNCAN   I'll tell Anne. You and Janie.

LOUIS   I could have had a dozen reasons for stopping by there. Besides, a fella will say anythin and everythin when he's... .

DUNCAN   You said. *(pause)* Anne never said. I know.

                Pause.

LOUIS   The thing is though... Anne doesn't care anymore. She's beat down. Maybe she doesn't say everythin she means. Y'know how sad she is all the time now. You want to make things happy for Anne.

DUNCAN   I know she said. I know. My sister.

LOUIS   Ya think so?

DUNCAN   I know her.

                Pause.

LOUIS   Yeah. I think ya think ya do.

Pause.

DUNCAN I'm not goin anywhere.

Silence.

LOUIS You know what's happenin. You're breakin her heart. You're killin her. Is that what ya want?

DUNCAN I love her.

LOUIS Ya can't! Ya can't! Cause it's clear. Clear as fuckin day.... There's some people than can survive... that can live... that can *abide*. Ya don't love her at all. If ya did, ya wouldn't be puttin her through hell every day! I see ya walkin back an forth across the highway. Ya know how many times I seen that? Back an forth to Mackie's, down the school, gettin an eyeful, teasin the dogs. back and forth across that road like you're some kinda fuckin bird... some kinda mother duck. Ya ever look both ways?

DUNCAN I always look both ways crossin over the road.

LOUIS Bullshit! Ya *never* look both ways. I watch ya! What should we do? Put up a fuckin sign, Duncan? A fuckin retard crossing sign? Is that what we should do?

DUNCAN I don't have to... I don't want to...

LOUIS You don't wanna you don't have to what?

DUNCAN I don't want to be retarded no more!

Pause.

LOUIS Is that so.

DUNCAN No more.

Silence.

LOUIS	Well. Life deals some shitty fuckin cards an you got the joker too bad so sad how the hell ya gonna *like* it if your sister looks out the window some day... sees a big red stain on the road... she loses the rest of what she's got cause you had to get your retarded pervert head smashed by a car because you couldn't follow the basic fuckin rules of civilization... she said this to me, Duncan. She said this to me... swear to God... she said she'd rather see you in Selby however much ya hate it than see you arrested sent to Nova Scotia hospital for life or run down like an animal...
DUNCAN	I know, Louis.
LOUIS	What?
DUNCAN	I know Anne.
LOUIS	I'm sure ya know her. Cause for all I know our baby's gonna be born just like you. Diseased in the fuckin mind. Just like you. It's in the blood!
DUNCAN	I'm sorry.
LOUIS	The hell ya are. It's not fair, Duncan. What am I supposed to do? *(pause)* There used to be such a thing as mercy.

Pause.

DUNCAN	Louis.
LOUIS	What?
DUNCAN	God works in mysterious ways.

Silence. LOUIS reaches for the bottle.

LOUIS	Alright. Have it your way.
DUNCAN	Louis...?
LOUIS	Pathetic. Some fuckin family...

DUNCAN	I'm tired now.
LOUIS	Bet everyone slept in the same big...
DUNCAN	Let's go home now.
LOUIS	Happy bed... whee...

Silence.

DUNCAN	Louis. I can't go to Selby.
LOUIS	Yeah. I know what ya did.

Pause.

Tried to hang yourself, eh?

Pause.

Well. Takes guts to try to hang yourself.

Pause.

I'd have to be drunk to try to hang myself.

LOUIS drinks.

The sun is setting.

— • — Scene 6 — • —

Twilight.

DUNCAN is fighting the onset of sleep. LOUIS stares out over the field.

LOUIS	Sleepy are ya? *(pause)* SLEEPY ARE YA.
DUNCAN	I'm awake.

LOUIS drinks.

LOUIS	Have another slug.
DUNCAN	No thanks.

Pause.

LOUIS	This field... the bare patch... used to be a paradise, Duncan. Moose... place was littered with whitetails. Even a few caribou still around. *(pause)* Like some kinda sanctuary. They'd come right up to you. No fear at all.

DUNCAN wakes momentarily.

DUNCAN	Yeah.
LOUIS	Mother an I up here pickin blueberries... come into this field... whole fuckin herd of white tails. Didn't run. Just looked at us like we were just another kind of animal. A whole gorgeous herd of them. *(pause)* They stayed there all afternoon with us just eatin the grass while me an her, we picked four quarts of berries. Yeah. *(pause)* Then me and the old man and Mackie and the Chinaman and some friend of the Chinaman come back up the next day and got six of them. Everyone guttin at the same time. Blood over the grass. We were drenched in it. *(pause)* That was my first.

Pause.

Then we ate venison in the middle of August with blueberry pie for dessert and no one knew a fuckin thing about it. No one saw a thing that day, did they? *(pause)* No one saw a thing.

Pause.

DUNCAN	*(half-asleep)* Mm...
LOUIS	*(laughs)* Duncan's gotta get his beauty rest. Pretty enough for Anne, though.
DUNCAN	*(half-asleep)* Anne.

Silence. LOUIS speaks very softly.

LOUIS   You're sufferin. I know you're sufferin. Cut off from a decent life. Punished in an awful way for some random reason. You're sufferin. It'll only get worse. On and on. I know.

Pause.

I know the lay of the land.

LOUIS reaches for his rifle.

DUNCAN   Wha?

LOUIS   I'm movin over cross the field. Maybe spook one.

DUNCAN   Where.

LOUIS   Over there. You wait here.

DUNCAN   It's gettin dark.

LOUIS   I know. We're goin home soon.

DUNCAN   I want to go with you.

LOUIS   No. You stay.

Pause. LOUIS takes a drink.

DUNCAN   Louis.

LOUIS   Here... I'll leave you the flashlight.

DUNCAN   Don't.

LOUIS   It's alright. I'll be back in a little while.

Pause.

DUNCAN   Anne loves you.

LOUIS   Fine. Alright then.

DUNCAN	Stay here.
LOUIS	Nothin to be scared of.
DUNCAN	I don't want to...
LOUIS	Christ! Stop it!

Pause.

DUNCAN	Okay. Louis.

Silence.

LOUIS	You see anyone you remember what the story is. And yell over to me. Got that?
DUNCAN	Joe... Curious.
LOUIS	Yeah. Good ol Joe.

LOUIS takes a drink and disappears.

It is becoming night. Rustling noises in the trees.

— • — Scene 7 — • —

Split scene.

Night. At first only DUNCAN is seen in the moonlight, sitting on the log. The flashlight is beside him. LOUIS is gradually seen on the distant other side of the field, the back of the theatre. He shoulders his rifle, aiming at DUNCAN.

There are rustling sounds in the surrounding forest, as it comes to life.

DUNCAN	Remember the story. This is it you see someone. Our father who art in heaven. Some fuckin saint of the mountain. We went for a walk in the woods. It was bleedin. On earth and in heaven...

LOUIS battles his demons, steeling himself with every action. Sliding the safety. Positioning the sights. DUNCAN reaches in his vest pocket and takes out shells. One by one, he loads them into the magazine of his shotgun.

I carry the shells. From the hardware. We followed the blood but we lost the trail. Gotta bring down that wounded deer. Wounded deer spreads disease. On and on. Give us this day our daily bread. Forgive us our trespasses. Point a gun at someone. We came here to fix a problem.

Silence.

The devil comes... deliver us...

DUNCAN rises and points his gun across the field.

Lights fade. A rifle shot booms in the dark. DUNCAN screams. He fires.

Another shot. Silence. Darkness.

The sound of a large animal, in death throes. Several shots in rapid succession.

—•— Scene 8 —•—

More shots. Still dark. The lights flash to black. Disorientation, total confusion in the massacre.

The shadow of a large buck, its antlers create giant stabbing shadows.

LOUIS   *(fires)* Twelve fuckin points on him.

DUNCAN   LOUIS...!

LOUIS   Twelve fuckin points on him EASY!

DUNCAN   IT'S A DEER, LOUIS!

LOUIS	He's comin toward you, Duncan! Give it to him!
	LOUIS fires.
DUNCAN	Give it to him! Safety... safe...
LOUIS	DON'T WAIT. HE'S COMIN RIGHT AT YA!
DUNCAN	I'm safe...
LOUIS	NOW! HE'S RIGHT ON FUCKIN TOP A YA, DUNCAN! SHOOT!
DUNCAN	Now.
	DUNCAN fires.
LOUIS	SHOOT!
DUNCAN	*(fires)* GIVE IT TO HIM! *(fires)* GIVE IT TO HIM!
LOUIS	ATTABOY!
DUNCAN	*(scream)* GIVE IT TO HIM!
LOUIS	ATTABOY... HE'S FALLING...!
DUNCAN	*(fires)* GIVE IT TO HIM...
LOUIS	HE'S DOWN! YA DID IT!
	Silence. The light rises on a dead bleeding deer in front of DUNCAN. LOUIS approaches, exultant.
	Ya did it, Duncan! I can't believe...
	DUNCAN stares at the corpse of the deer.
DUNCAN	Don't worry your pretty little head about it.
LOUIS	Look what we did. You slaughtered him. Nailed him three times right in the neck. There's one of mine in the shoulder. No need to bleed this fella.

DUNCAN   (*pause*) Attaboy.

LOUIS   Wait till we show everyone what ya did. I taught ya, didn't I? Who woulda thought you could ever...! Ah, you're some piece a work you are! You're the man! I never knew ya had this... Duncan...!

DUNCAN   I'm safe.

> *LOUIS, blood on his hands, approaches DUNCAN. DUNCAN's rifle is pointed at LOUIS. Pause.*

LOUIS   Where'd you get... I never gave you any...

> *DUNCAN looks at him. LOUIS understands. DUNCAN looks back at the corpse. LOUIS looks at him.*
>
> *He lays down his rifle away from the spreading pool of blood. A gesture of peace. Perhaps surrender. DUNCAN lays his rifle down also. Their eyes never leave each other.*

DUNCAN   Give me... the knife.

LOUIS   Huh?

> *Pause.*

DUNCAN   We have to bring the heart back.

> *LOUIS passes him the knife. He watches, with admiration and fear, as DUNCAN cuts into the dead animal.*
>
> *Blackout.*

photo by John Hillis

MICHAEL MELSKI is an award-winning writer and filmmaker from Cape Breton. His many stage plays including *Joyride* and *Heartspent and Black Silence* have been produced across Canada. He was playwright-in-residence at the Shaw Festival and published in *Blood on Steel: Two Plays*. His *Hockey Mom, Hockey Dad* has toured nationally to packed audiences across Canada, and was published by Breton Books. His play *Miles From Home* was a smash hit in the summer of 2001, breaking box office records at Ship's Company Theatre. In the 2002 Nova Scotia Theatre Awards, he was nominated twice in the Best Play category. His other plays include *A Sense of Direction* and *Hello from Sirius*. He is currently writing *The Trout Fisher's Companion*, a new play commissioned by Ship's Company Theatre.

Michael has been called "A Great Writer" (David Adams Richards), "An Important New Voice in Canadian Fiction" (*Atlantic Books Today*) and one of "100 Canadians To Watch" by *Macleans*. He is thirty-three years old, and divides his time between Halifax and Toronto.